WALKING WITH BOTH FEET

WALKING WITH BOTH FEET

Editor
Catherine Allan

This book is dedicated to all those who helped make it

Designed by:
Jo Caryl at CARAD
with Catherine Allan

CARAD

POWYS MENTAL HEALTH ALLIANCE
CHYNGRAIR IECHYD MEDDYLIOL POWYS

Published by:
Powys Mental Health Alliance
Worcester House, Temple Street, Llandrindod Wells,
Powys LD1 5DU. Tel: 01597 825593

ISBN 0-9541306-0-X
Printed in Ireland by
Colourbooks Ltd.

Foreword

I'm very happy to be able to write an introduction for this book as this is just the sort of project that I think is very valuable and rarely acknowledged as such, because it is on a comparatively small scale. (As someone on a comparatively big scale, small has always appealed!)

I have always enjoyed writing, particularly poetry and found it to be a medium which most profoundly expresses the deepest feelings we all have ... or the silliest for that matter.

As an ex-psychiatric nurse for ten years working in an economically deprived area of South London, I am well aware of the continuing huge stigma attached to those who suffer mental health problems and the fact that in this throwaway, fast moving society most ordinary people are just not encouraged to express their feelings, let alone those who have suffered emotionally.

So I say, good on you and congratulations to all those contributors. I hope this is a resounding success.

Very, very, very good luck.

Jo Brand

Acknowledgements

EDITING TEAM
Sincere thanks to the following co-editors:
Pat Atkinson, Ruth Bemment, Cynthia Mullan, Philip Pashley, Robin Wilson

WRITING WORKSHOP LEADERS:
Pat Atkinson, Elizabeth Griffiths, Chris Kinsey, Angela Morton, Philip Pashley

ILLUSTRATION WORKSHOPS and front cover illustration:
Esme Corfield

PHOTOGRAPHY WORKSHOPS:
Steve Jones and Dave Woods at CARAD, Community Arts Rhayader and District

Groups contributing to the publication:
Brecon and District Contact Group,
Mid Powys MIND,
Ponthafren Association,
The Triangle Group,
US MACH,
Ysradgynlais
Community Contact Group.

We gratefully acknowledge the assistance of:

celf o gwmpas

arts around about

Celf o Gwmpas who administer Powys Mental Health's Arts for All Lottery grant in partnership with the Arts Promotion Group of Powys Mental Health Alliance.

Richard Davies
Parthian Books, Cardiff.

Joanne Nixon

Funded by an 'Arts For All' Lottery grant from the
Arts Council of Wales

CRONFA LOTERI
LOTTERY FUND

CYNGOR
CELFYDDYDAU
CYMRU

THE ARTS
COUNCIL
OF WALES

Introduction

This book has come about as a result of workshops held in Mental Health Drop In centres throughout Powys. Funded by an 'Arts For All' Lottery grant from the Arts Council of Wales, the workshops were organised in conjunction with Powys Mental Health Alliance and Celf o Gwmpas.

Most of the people who have contributed to the book have, from time to time, experienced various levels of mental illness or emotional distress. Recovery from or stabilising an illness or emotional distress is often achieved by the right medical treatment and by support from friends and family.

However, a large part of being able to recover is being able to regain a sense of self-esteem and a feeling of being in control of their lives. Being able to express one's creativity is one of the most satisfying routes to that end.

It has been a privilege to meet and work with contributors. I have been astounded and moved by their honesty and by what has been produced under sometimes near impossible or deeply distressing circumstances.

Catherine Allan
Editor

Contents

in alphabetical order of first names page no

Ruth

Adam

There is a photo somewhere taken on the day
you were born to Joe and Becky.
I was so thin and my hair, uncut for so long,
tumbles about my face and down my back where
it lies like a rope against my tense spine.
I was still ill when you came to us, but out of
hospital at last.
All those pills made me tense and shaky but
your mummy said,
"Come on Mum, come and hold him."
We made a safe place for me to sit so that I had
a nest in my lap for you.

I was afraid you would start to cry when you
were in my jerky arms. I felt the down of your
head against my skin, I smelt your new-born
smell, I felt your warmth and weight and I forgot
my unwell self as I cradled you. And you lay
warm and peaceful in my arms, and then I saw
the little frown between your brows begin to
ease, your eyelids flickered and then opened and
you looked at me with your blue eyes, your wise
blue eyes.

You looked at me with calm, and peace and then
I sensed a wisdom in you, a wisdom you had
brought with you from somewhere else, some
other world inhabited in other time, in other
space, from where you'd left behind nearly all
that you once were but some faint trace of
memory born on the wings of love.

Angela Morton

Birth Of A Generation

She was rolling in clover,
For it was almost over.
She was every woman
That delivered,
And her baby was every baby
That shivered.
She touched a somewhere
New to her, yet she knew
It had always been there,
Forever surrounding her.
She was every woman
Given up to pain,
For all the gain
Of every birth.
Agony gave way to mirth,
Involuntary scream of effort
To yells of delight.
Holding newness in her arms,
Feeding this bundle with her
charms,
Milk of human kindness,
oblation,
Nourishing honey for next
generation.
Mother of all the earth,
She embraced her worth.
One hand in eternity,
One hand in time,
A vessel living on borderline.

Judith Thomas

My favourite present was when I was eleven. I watched my baby brother being born. It was scary for a moment as he turned blue but when his colour came back and I heard his just scream and saw his little hands and feet, he looked so beautiful.

Robin Wilson

My Earliest Memories

Salt, sour milk and plaster dust. I remember dimly being trapped inside a kind of coffin of plaster. The truth is that the ceiling of my nursery fell in during an air raid and I was only preserved for this life by the lathes of the ceiling falling across my cot and the powdery, dusty age old plaster drifting like lumpy snow into my face, my nose, my ears, my nappy.
The taste and smell of old buildings still involve a prickly, scary feeling of hair standing in fear.

Anona

Baby's Feet

New,
        as yet untested by the burden of life.
Innocent, fresh, sweet smelling,
                                        pink perfection.

Ten mini digits open to sensory exploration,
With luck this child shall grow into adulthood well grounded.
        Earthed by their unshod feet,
Their sole always open to life's rich experiences,
Standing upright in all their glory,
                                        Well balanced.

Carol Loud

Esme Corfield

Garden Peas

Boiling peas and Brussels
sprouts simmer and let off a
steam that fights with the
windowpanes.
The frosted glass seems
to cocoon us.
I sit thinking
of the
boredom of
October
Sundays and
why, when
you're small, sprouts are never
out of season.
The football rages on the
television then simmers down.
I hide behind the sofa and await
some action.

Tracey Friel

Martin

Loneliness Aged Four

Who is this four year old girl?
She stands and stares
Through the large French window
Does she say her prayers?
Is this nursery cheerful and happy?
With its scattering of toys
Is she lost in a world on her own
Or with other girls and boys?
Along one wall is a massive fire
Is it red and cosy bright?
Does it send fingers of warmth and cheer?
Is everything all right?

One day all cloudy and dark
She sits in this room so stark
Today she's a little cold and sick
She needs someone to help her, be quick
But who is there to listen
As her tears begin to glisten
Can the rag doll in the corner speak?
Can the tin soldier kiss her cheek?
Can the teddy give her a hug?
NO
What she needs beside her on the rug
Is human companionship and love
And God's eternal caring from above.

Sue

Esme Corfield

What's in the yoghurt pot?

"Here you are, it's a pressy for you." I said, handing her a yoghurt tub from my grubby hands. She smiled and put it on the windowsill in the kitchen.
"You will look after them mummy, you will give them some dinner."
"Yes - now for goodness sake's go and get washed, take off your boots and wash all that smelly mud off yourself."
I never saw the tadpoles again. My poor tadpoles probably ended up down the loo - I could never please my mother on Mother's Day.

Anona

Tangnefedd

A word dredged from boyhood
from hymns in cold chapel,
distant masters with stern faces
sitting like judges, scanning
the hosts of mouthing boys,
black caps ready for sentence.
Peace, one of the many words
to be seen to be spoken
and which I did not understand.

Tangnefedd. Had I realised its
beauty then -
would it have been so easily lost?

Len Thomas

The Circle

Sadly I dressed each morning,
And as I walked to school,
I knew that what I had to face
Was being made a fool.
They did not speak a word to
me.
I knew not what I'd done.
Before it started I loved school.
I found it so much fun.
In the playground it was hell,
For there it struck with force.
They circled round me, jeering,
And they seemed strong, of
course.
I was centre of the circle,
And they pushed me round.
How could I stand this moment
When I fell down to the ground.

But all this happened years ago,
And I have come to know
There is a greater Circle
Around me as I grow.
So my past has not hurt me
In fact it's made me strong.
The Circle that protects me
Is God's Love where I belong.

Judith Thomas

Snow

Empty snowy virgin paths
waiting to be walked on, so
clean bright and beautiful
reflecting blue skies, dazzling
to the eye.
Black rooftops billowing out
their smoke of fires lit in
fireplaces below.
Hills that only a few days ago
were covered in assorted
colours of green, now white with
snow.
Cows and sheep grazing on
bales of hay, that farmers grew
back earlier in the year.
Such peace, but hark! What do I
hear, the peace and quiet
shattered with the joy and
laughter of children with
sledges and children with
makeshift sledges made from
old rubbish bags slipping and
sliding down the slopes, and
having a great time. Snowball
fights ensuing. Shrieks of
horror as a snowball catches
one child right on the back of
the neck, cold wet snow slipping
down their back as they stand
up, but quickly getting over the
initial shock they bend down to
gather the soft snow up in their
hands to throw back.
Holly bushes bursting forth with
enough berries to feed all the
hungry birds. Squirrels busy
gathering enough nuts to see
them through the winter days,
praying that it does not freeze
over.
At the end of the day, snow
falling covering the tracks,
made earlier in the day.
Snowmen sitting in gardens, so
alone each one unique, all
different shapes and sizes,
created with fun and laughter.
In the distance the sound of
laughter breaks the stillness of
the evening, adults now
enjoying what they are
embarrassed to enjoy in the
light of day, being the child
once again, even if only for a
short time.
At last all is quiet. Now the
animals, the cats, playing and
falling into drifts of snow, trying
to clamber out, eventually they
make it to play once again.
Snow has stopped falling,
moonlight and stars shine down
onto the snow-covered land
below.

Margaret Hardman

Esme Corfield

Scarlet Knickers

Saturday afternoon and once again, I'm sat under the wooden picnic chairs eating rice crispy cakes, cross legged, at the jumble sale. Behind me, Mrs Mariot in her tweed matching twin-set, is trying to discreetly wipe the pink lipstick off the side of the green cup she has been drinking from. She seems as interested in her conversation as I am in jumble sales. Occasionally she looks up at her opponent and gives a false smile.

Directly in front of me, all I see are people's feet shuffling and snow melting from their shoes leaving sludgy puddles behind. The door swings open and a cold blast sends goose bumps up my arm. Buzzing voices hum about the room, children shout and giggle. A noise like a Gatling gun spins past as children play a game of tick. At the table busy mums are pushing their way into the bargains regarding items and holding them clear or discarding them. Children hunt around the miscellaneous stall where small glass jars, beads and other strange treasures lie waiting to be discovered.

Husbands wait in corners loaded up with bags, staring at the floor and admiring their watches.

Surely she's bought the whole sale out by now? I stare out of the high windows wondering how to pass the time. I decide to open my blue fizzy pop. It makes a spitting noise and sticky pop drips up my arms. I shake my sleeve but it doesn't do the trick. I'm wet all the way up to my elbow.

My patience is dying quickly, I've run out of crispy cakes and I'm all sticky. Some old ladies have sat above me, one of them I recognise as Mrs Mariot. She's sat on my chair. I look up at the wooden slats on the chair; they seem to bend in the middle. They're not small ladies and I begin to fear for my safety. Thankfully, mum pays for her goods and is making for the door, but, as she turns I find its not mum at all, just another lady wearing a pink top and blue jeans.

I rest my elbows on my knees and pray that the chair holds out.

I become disheartened as I realise mum might have been looking for me or even gone home. What's more, I couldn't climb from my hiding place now. I don't think it would be polite to climb out from under Mrs Mariot's legs.

I start to notice the ladder going up Mrs Mariot's tights; it grows every time she crosses her legs. The hall becomes quieter as people file out and I can hear the tittle tattle going on above me.
"He didn't did he?"
"I've looked after him since he was a child and he was a terror then. Those that are good natured children are always pleasant adults."
"There's just no telling some people, why they do these things, I'll never know, and in public, how embarrassing."

Suddenly the chair cracks, a giant split has appeared in the woodwork. It spreads further and further along the chair. I hold my breath. Snap. Half the chair collapses. I scream. Mrs Mariot screams. The hall is full of silent spectators and I crawl from under the chair. Mrs Rollins and Mrs Thomson try to pull Mrs Mariot from the wreckage. Through the huffing and puffing only I can see that the tweed skirt is caught by the wooden slat of the chair. With one big heave, Mrs Mariot is on her feet and the skirt remains on the floor. The entire hall bursts into a fit of giggles at the sight of her scarlet knickers.

Tracey Friel

Things In A Box

Toffees
Tiny pieces of marble
Tiny sparkling diamonds
6 dried peas
1/2 oz of lentils

2 horse bolts
3 dice
3 two pence pieces
3 pearls
Small jigsaw pieces
Pebbles

Mrs Clare Barnard
Aged 26

Rainbow Child

When I was little, my mum would
say,
What colour of the rainbow will
you be today?
I do know sometimes I drove her
wild,
Maybe that's why she called me,
her rainbow child.

If I got angry, I'd turn quite red,
Throw things around, then she'd
send me to bed.
I didn't like bulls, I was scared of
their bellow,
And just like a coward, I'd feel I
was yellow.

When fit as a fiddle, I'd be "in the pink,"
And my lovely complexion make little boys wink!
Sometimes I'd get envious, didn't want to be seen,
'Cause nobody fancied a girl that turned green!

Look out when I raged and scared lots of people,
For the monster that shrieked was me, I'd be purple!
On the days I was sad, didn't know what to do,
I needed a cuddle, didn't like being blue.

I nearly forgot one, the hardest of all,
Well, could you describe orange, when you were small?
I would rack my brains; 'till I dizzied my head,
Then decided, I'd peel it, and eat it instead!

Bobbie Davies

The Children At Llangattock 6 a.m.

The children are awake
these noisy pups of peace
I groan and then
seek amnesty with them
needing no flag of truce,
I shrug off guilt
and join their games,
for gladness happens rarely.

Len Thomas

Doggies

The doggies held a meeting
They came from miles around
They came from every private home
They came from every pound.
Each doggy passed the entrance
Each doggy signed the book
Then all unzipped his own behind
And hung it on the hook.
One doggy was not invited
It sorely raised his ire
He ran into the meeting hall
And loudly bellowed FIRE.
It threw them in confusion
And without a second look
Each grabbed another's behind
From off another's hook.
And that's the reason why
When doggies chance to meet
And that's the reason why
When walking down the street
On land or sea or foam
A dog will sniff another's behind
To see if it is their own.

Bob Lewis

Robin Wilson

A Dog's Tale

I once had a dog called Sandy who was adored by me and a lady called Mandy who was very handy on her tandem.
She would take Sandy with her to play ball.
Sandy would jump and land with a bump, but something distracted Sandy when his eyes met a poodle called Gandi.
Sandy got very randy when he met Gandi.
"You naughty boy" shouted Mandy but Sandy and Gandi were in puppy heaven and couldn't give a tiddle wink.

Robin Wilson

Belle

Soft velvet nose nuzzling warmly
big brown eyes full of wisdom
strong neck to catch me if I fall
wide back to carry my burdens
four feet planted firmly on the ground
silky tail carried high with pride.

Amanda Wells

A Foreign Place

I am in a very warm foreign place. The sea is bright turquoise colour. It is very hot, the sunshine on the turquoise sea is casting warm shades of orange, red and yellow. Like it is being intertwined with the turquoise. There are hills in the distance and an island jutting out from the piece of land I am sitting on. I am sitting on a mahogany-coloured log. There are a couple of trees on the land. The undergrowth is a mass of colour. Blues, purples, reds, pinks, aquamarines, yellows, orange and mahogany. The hills in the distance look like striking navy blue and turquoise.

The island is a striking royal blue, with green and red intertwined with it like gorse. Only more effective than you would see in Britain.

I am wearing a cool linen hat and a white cardigan to deflect the heat. The land is so dry under foot, it crunches like dry twigs snapping, but it is not twigs but old leaves; it is dusty too. A slapping sound echoes, as I brush the dust from my well maintained walking boots and trousers.

The smell of the sea is fresh and salty. I can taste the salt on my lips and I actually had a gentle spray of the waves, as they caress the shore. I brush my cheeks and they taste slightly of salt. The sun is getting hotter as the day goes on.

Mo Steele

Ruth

"A Fine Cornish Day"

It is 11.00am on a mild Monday morning.
Birds sing overhead.
The reeded wicker washing basket is creaking,
as clothing is being removed from it.
There are boats sailing on the calm sea.
There are birds flying around overhead.
Wind gently blows at the washing.
A young woman is retrieving washing from the
creaky washing basket.
Washing is placed neatly on the stone wall to dry.
There are geese pecking around for food
amongst the short tufts of grass.
A water barrel is still collecting droplets of water
from the rain shower from the day before.
It is Springtime.
There is an island on the left hand side
of the picture.
It is golden yellow.
On the island is stone intertwined with foliage.
"Which bit of washing should I put
on the line next?"
The woman asks herself.
"Thank goodness there is not a fox about!"
It is dark on the other side of the world,
otherwise, it would not be daylight in my picture.

Mo Steele

Horizons

Whenever I spread my pack of art cards
you pick Richard Wanes's *Washing Day*.

Is it the vision of balance,
the woman's ability to hinge from her hip
dip straight-backed to her basket
and gather linens whiter than the grazing
ducks?

Or is there another frame -
you both straighten with ease, stretch to the line
pause before pegging, gaze past gorse cliffs,
past sails to where sea inks a line under white
sky?

Chris Kinsey

A Woman In Hard Times

It is late evening and I've been ironing and scrubbing for eighteen hours and I am feeling extremely tired, my shoulders and arms are aching with pain. I hear the Landlord snore, and it makes me feel even more tired. I try to imagine I'm lying on the beach in the lovely hot weather, licking an ice cream. Then I wake up and I'm back in hell. My head drooping with tiredness and I try to keep my eyes open as I can hardly move. I am twenty three years old my name's Kathleen Mary Gee Wilmot and I look and feel more like ninety-three. It is 1912 and I hear the news on the Cat's Whisker that the Titanic has been hit by an iceberg and has sunk.

Robin Wilson

Industry, Waterloo

(Based On A Picture By Monet)

Rome, London, Paris to Venice, Claude Monet had a difficult trip. See it in his expression, comprehend, understand. The daughter of the pit later collected his beautiful works. The gardener could never survive. Falling through the smog, just like Tiger Bay, he would go back to France or beyond, had enough of falsities.

Even during the Industrial, you can see calm water flooding into the sea of peace.

The brush strokes of colour. He was in a rush. This is new to us, the Davis collection. Would they want this one? Even during those times there was slavery.

Beauty is only a vision that we conceive. So if you conceive the inconceivable, you have conceived it. If you don't conceive the inconceivable, it cannot be. So don't conceive the inconceivable so if you can't conceive the inconceivable it cannot be conceived, if you conceive it, it is conceived. So don't conceive the inconceivable.

Zac

Sunshine

Summer is the time of year for sunshine.
The countryside is abundant with fragrant flowers.
Ramblers set off for cross-country walks.
Parties arrange different bus trips.
Sitting in the shade and breeze with a glass of lemonade.
Watching the kingfishers by the canal.
Children with candy floss and ice cream.
Sitting on the beach watching "Punch and Judy" shows.
Camping outdoors up on the mountains, near a running stream and tins of beans and sausages at hand.

Helen

Man V/S Nature

Heaven covered earth in petals of winter.
Houses crouched under the heavy emptying sky.
Gusty winds swirled flakes into shapes of infinite diversity.
But the fields were empty of life as the naked trees held their branches to the sky.
Neither bird nor beast entered the scene.

The peace was destroyed as the inanimate object revved noisily.
Refusing containment, the metallic box defiantly pressed forward with busy wipers removing the nuisance from its screen,
seeking escape to another milieu of bright lights, warm air, and canned music to hypnotise and deaden the senses. A world where polystyrene bodies are shrouded in gaudily dyed nylon, and security guards protect the consumer consumables.
Man's world, where nature is impotent.

But the car has not reached there. The wind swirls around it,
gently pushing it from is precarious course.
It swerved - is rebuffed by a tree, rebounds and turns over.
Scarlet drops stain the whiteness.
Now it is silent and Heaven continues to cover the earth in petals of winter.

Ruth

Purple Peacocks

Pink fire works, Venice, the Gondola, Monet's
perception, beauty of natural impressionism,
the gold oak, the copper beach, amber leaves,
briskly falling.
The boat shaped moon. Champagne eyes,
Gimme a mince pie.
Purple ways, such a wonderful day.

Zac

Bike

Push those pedals and freak out, loose yourself in the right gear, keep it in the same gear. Blow your mind full of fresh air, combustion off the calories.

Trip up the main street knowing the breathalyser will touch you not and driving licence credential is non-exist. Fart as much as you like, you're on the move so nobody's nostril can blame you.

All you need is balance and a degree in the behaviour of the Highway Code. Just don't run anyone down, in particular old ladies and young children, but have a go at the rest, provided you're insured.

There again, let's get things into perspective. You've only got a pushbike that doesn't go far because you will inherit a sore arse.

Gina

Toils Heritage

They toiled in most men's cases
In those fathoms for black gold
'Till limbs ached and their faces
The pathetic story told.

Many yearned for lands distant
Where greener grasses grew
Forsaking pick and Davy lamp
In search of pastures new

Some found solace in
New England
Or assisted passage sought
To the colony "down-under"
Where the mineshaft was of
nought

Many stayed in Wales to fight
Not only for the coal
But for the basic human right
To sustain heart and soul.

For heritage so dear today
Of which all Welsh partake
Render heartfelt thanks to those
Who did our platform make.

Phil Brown

Porthcawl

In the summer John went to Porthcawl
There were rides at the fair - John tried them all
His favourite the dodgems and the Rollacoaster ride
When John finished he went inside…
…Inside a Restaurant, John had a big meal
The Bacon, Sausage, Egg and Chips was simply unreal
At 6.30 it was goodbye to Porthcawl
John caught the bus back to Brenton Hall!!
John And Friends

Porthcawl By The Sea

I'd like to go to Porthcawl in a Bright Blue Car
I'd need plenty of fuel because to walk is too far
I'd go with Nicky because she's staying with me
Down to Porthcawl, down by the sea.
I'd go with Nicky because she's staying with me
We'd go down to Porthcawl, by the sea.
Tracy And Friends

The Big Yellow Taxi

In a Big Yellow Taxi we drove off to town
We went up a hill and then we came down
Trees, Fields and Mountains - Welsh Countryside
Tracy and John came along for the ride
We arrived in Brecon, John said he'd pay
We got out of the taxi and went on our way
Along to the Punch Bowl, the Siddons - Boars Head
Drinking far to much beer – 'Time to go,' Tracy said
So in a Big Yellow Taxi we drove out of town
We went up a hill and then we came down
Trees, Fields and Mountains - Welsh Countryside
Tracy and John came along for the ride.
Mark And Friends

The Barbecue

It was a hot day - the sky was blue
Chris, Gemma, Marilyn (and friends) held a barbecue
So much food, salad, chicken, lots of meat
There was plenty for everyone to eat
Chris started singing Spirit in the Sky
Why Spirit in the Sky? She didn't know why
Yes Chris she was singing Spirit in the Sky
When there's another Barbecue you want to give it a try
Chris And Friends

The Lakes

Tracy said she would like to go to the Lakes
On one of those Holiday - Activity breaks
She'd like to go for more than just a weekend
At least seven days - with a friend
Chris and Tracy would walk in the mountains
They'd both sail on the lakes
When they go on one of those Holiday - Activity breaks!
Tracy And Friends

The Thunderbird Bus

I remember my first ride on the Blue Thunderbird Bus
My Mother and Father said I caused such a fuss
I made a noise, I started a row
But I'm older so I don't do it now
On that day we ran out of petrol
But I had a big tin
So they sent me to the garage
And a man put some in
Yes we started in Llangynidr went up a ridge
Down through Brecon onto Sennybridge
I remember my first ride on the Blue Thunderbird Bus
My Mother and Father said I caused such a fuss
John And Friends

A Sense Of three Different Places

I see myself in Tooting high road, and in Radnor on shepherd's mound, also at Borth beach.

Tooting high road, there are three and a half thousand people walking up and down an ordinary city main road and pavement and they are shopping. I mean real shopping not standing around arguing with the husband and wife, about whatever.
They were walking into all the up town names, Dixons, Curry's, Jean Jeannie, purchasing a lot of stuff. More queues outside of banks. 2.00 p.m. in the afternoon, and battleship grey.

In front of me I see an ice age creation, high hills and low flat moraine valleys.
Rush with grass grazed on by Texel ewes and rams. We are situated on top of a grave from Roman times. God above saw all it, creation in ice age, bottles and death, numerous invasions. 4.00 p.m. in the day. Light is harsh and sticking. I am at the highest point with more Gods and more land.

We are a low tide near Aberystwyth, the sand is deeply yellow and the tides ebb over a lot of shale and pebbles. A lone windsurfer goes by, followed by courageous kids yelling, pointing, hurriedly.

I am with a black man and his white wife and one of their children. His wife and myself are extremely overweight. But when you're fat, God can't be found. There is an eligible beauty usually with the health crisis it causes, and with the bits over examined and held in and the way clothes fit after drying.

A golf course and a lone ice cream shop. 2.00 p.m. in the afternoon. Extremely bright and shining like a UFO.

I am waiting for Michael to catch up as I walk up the steep slope. Suddenly he stops and sends up a cloud of smoke from a cigarette and paces on.

I am waiting for No. 361 bus in Tooting. Every minute another and another comes, each time I ask, "Next one," the conductor replies, as hordes of people cut in and out of the buses at the stop. I see mine coming sixty yards at away. Will it be full?

I am waiting for a towel or beach cover to get out of my leg cut short jeans. The longer I wait, the more an argument breaks out. One in creation must have left and rocked the assurance away. I'm still waiting for beach cover. C'mon, c'mon.

Immediately the bus driver sees me, waves and passes, he's full. Mum turns and says, we can walk, it's only 40 minutes, or even less on the underground. The decision is left to me. I argue there are a lot of people around. Before I know it and after my advice, we both decide another bus would take us nearer.

Suddenly I jump, feel nervous. The wind is cascading the valley and we stand like draught extractors, the highest in Radnorshire. He then receives a mobile phone call, we're ordered to retreat and return home and I'm alone the whole time in my mind and people don't respond for days and days. Worry sets in, then ends its course.

The black man says, "you can wrap a bloody towel around yourself Ok. Trevor and you can get on with it, sucker." I'm glum inside.

Then the bus appears empty in five places, two hundred yards into our walk. We watch it. I am resentful as my mum is fairly old and needs and lift. And at the stop my brother another lift, another day to go nowhere, but he's friendly and we are amused by his wise cracks about his afternoon.

At the end of the weekend I realise things are desperate no one is communicating, we are down from the Bound, for days and days it drags on. That night, there is nothing to eat, just the cries of sheep and calves wanting feed. Suddenly in the morning, dad arrives. He's caught on and realises I'd been worked to death, un-fed and not to be approached. Immediately he started the car and we're off. I never let greed get control, many times I returned and some days were better than I thought.

At the time it occurs to me that I might never change, met obviously by the comments of, "What d'ya do eh, you was up all night, laughing at the cheese eh? Why don't ya figure melody for yourself." I dwell on my obesity and see I have no future in this state. Annoyingly I decide to end my position as a guest and start exercising daily for my own health.

The road is diverted, the police are swarming everywhere and armed soldiers - fire engines and

there are 26 million people who all ignore it. The bus driver ploughs on thinking of me, my mum and brother. He's dwelling on what part of London we sound like we're from. He decides his chances are about had, and finds someone else to dwell on.

When I arrive home it occurred to me that my dad laughed at me and began wondering if I'd lend a hand with our own business. I offered nothing, it's just a chance for dad to cause worry to my friends who will think that I have no time for them. I'm no help. Dad would pay but it's a chance to be church holy and in it I was heretically evil.

We leave, the black man is driving and the boy playing. I guess it's not all depression. I remember good and better under the protection of each other. In a moment we'll be home and the night closes in. I fall asleep with the whirr and thud of the interior of the car.

Trevor Lewis

There is a chill wind in the air
memories of the summer are fading.
The evenings grow ever shorter
but the autumn colours that brighten up
the often dull days are soon blown away.
And the stark reality of winter stares us in the face.
Every season has its special charm
and autumn is I feel, a proud season.

Peter Pickford

Feels Like Endless Waiting

I am walking along a road, ahead of me is a tree in its full beauty with branches sprouting leaves of every green colour from dark green to almost yellow. There are a few elderly people walking their dogs and there are more trees glimmering in the sunlight reflecting on a huge white building that is of no use to anyone or anything. It's a building deserted by many years of no use. It used to be a hotel back in the year of 1898 then for many years it was used as an army hospital during the war but now it just stands empty. Behind me is a very steep hill with fields, sheep, cows and a railway line. A few roads branch off from this particular road, two branch off half way up, the other right at the top of the hill. On my right side I can see in the distance a sign saying waterfalls one mile. To my left there are huge hills immersed in sunlight occasionally being covered by the shadows of the floating white clouds. The sun is beaming down on me right now making me lovely and warm with a cool breeze in thebackground.

I am standing totally alone waiting for a friend to come from 200 miles away. She seems to be taking a long time to come. Will she come at all? Waiting goes on longer than expected. My heart is pounding with fear that my friend might not arrive or if she does, she will get here in one piece! My hands are sweating and shaking, my legs are aching and there is no seat at the bus shelter and the bus shelter is one mile away. I am still waiting. Ah! Here's a bus I wonder if that might be her after all. There is another seatless bus shelter further along the road in my sight. Brilliant the bus has stopped, I am running to the bus, I've only got a few more yards to go. Five minutes in I'm here.

"Camilla!"

"Oh, sorry, I thought you were someone I was expecting to see."

Damn, it's not her, looks like the waiting time is over, I'm feeling very depressed now. Why hasn't she come? I'm walking back to my first point in the road.

"Now hang on, I've just thought.

There might be one more bus."
I'll have a look at the timetable.
"Oh brilliant. There is another bus at 7.00pm the last one. Please God let her be on this next bus please!"
Ten minutes on:
"Right this is the last bus I'm keeping my fingers tightly crossed that she is here. Yes!"
She's here, I'm now breathing a sigh of relief that she's made it. I'm still going to ask her why she's late but I'm not as angry as I was when the last bus came.
"Camilla, Hi, it's so long since I last saw you, how are you? I've been waiting since 5 o'clock what happened to you?"
We are now in each other's arms, very pleased to see each other. Five minutes later we're walking towards my house three miles away. Camilla has just told me that the trains, all of them, were ten minutes late and she missed one connection and had to wait half an hour.
I told Camilla how I had planned to cook a meal but now it was getting into late evening we'd have a night out on the town instead, Chinese meal, a drink in the pub and a slow walk home. I didn't fancy cooking at 8.00pm in the evening. We've now spent a week together and I've invited her to stay for another seven weeks. Well, why not? She lives on her own, surrounded by smog, noisy traffic, air pollution and incinerators. She could well do without all of that and there are no hills and trees of health and beauty where she lives, nor animals or clean air. Yesterday we took an evening walk and as we went past a nearby farm we saw a cat giving birth to ten tiny kittens. We couldn't touch them of course, but seeing them was just as beautiful. Then we picked some flowers to take home with us.

Mrs Clare Barnard
Aged 26

Trees

Stand like the tree, stretch your body into life
Feeling positive, feeling wonderful
Full of energy, dance like the tree in the breeze.
Witchy trees swaying in the moonlight, eerie as the moon
Shines down on the earth aglow.
Cold freezing trees on a frosty white night, standing on
a grey white grass.
Happiest on a summer's day in the sun.
The tree then has its leaves and is at its best.
Blossoms blowing in the breeze as the warm sun
Touches its branches and trunk.
The tree dances like a life full of happiness and joy.

Sheila Perry

Mary-Jo

Georgian Harp Music:

Sunlight flickers through the trees,
golden notes of music dancing.
Cloaks billow in the breeze,
horses grand with graceful prancing.
Terriers dart here and there.
Kestrels search out their prey.
But the mood's a happy peaceful one on
this glorious summer's day.

Bold hunters' hearts aren't in the kill,
as along they merrily ride.
The stag is safe to rule his hill
but the rabbits dive to hide.
Stonechants, echoing the horses' hooves
flit amongst the rich and purple gorse.
The swifts' and swallows' rapid flight
seems to wing a giddy aimless course.

Wildflowers dance a last lazy minuet.
Larks lead the evening choir.
The crows present in silhouette,
Perched atop a cattle byre.
Their presence inharmonious
with the scene of peace and calm
but summer anoints the coming eve
with her warm and soothing balm.

Carole Bullock

Pauline Dean

When the sun sets and the moon is out,
we walk across the beach. I feel the water,
my hair is blowing, and we are holding hands.
As we walk along we talk together
as we are with each other and enjoying the time.
So I will remember it from my heart.

Sian

The Magical Forest

I would like to be under a tree
with a man to be with all the time,
so he will be with me.
It would be lovely to stay with him in the sun.
So I will hope to remember and to
hear the birds flying again to the sky and
to have some food under the tree and drink under the tree.
And the water flowing down from the tree
flowing down, and me and my man watching it
and holding hands together as we go apart from the tree.

Sian

‘A Forest Walk’

If I had my sandals on I’d have leaf
mould squelching through my toes by
now.
Green tunnels before, and behind. This
tree trunk feels warmer than I expected
and the barks softer.
Light playing peek a boo with the leaves
because if I say it’s diffused and
dappled, I won’t like it.
Oh shit, I hope that was a squirrel.
Something rippled by in the corner of
my eye - now it’s gone.
Leaving me all super sensitive.
Green tunnels behind and before,
leading me.

Jill Dibling

Leaves

Leaves of all shapes and sizes, all different colours
fluttering down on meadows and rivers.
Blown by the high winds on to byways and paths.
Swept down the tiny streams and brooks.
Forming an enchanted dance – the winds forming the
orchestra.
This is in winter months, but when spring comes along
there is a different tale.
Fresh new leaves take the place of old Autumn browns.
Soon the world becomes quite like a fairyland – all
fresh and green and a delight to the eye.

Helen

Ruth

The Waterfall

I picture myself at the foot of a great waterfall known as "Water Break its Neck"

1. I see the white water falling effortlessly and unceasingly, yet somehow wearing away at the living rock.

2. I see the lichen growing green on the moist rock, somehow nourished by whatever the water and rocks contain. It makes no noise, but it thrives here.

3. I also see the great gorge cut by the water itself over many centuries.

(This is a real place, in the forestry near New Radnor, I have been there and I have photographs of it.)

The light level suggests late evening and the limited flow of water indicates late summer, the ash trees in full leaf agree with this.

Michael D Lewis

25th July 2000

I am waiting for my girl friend to arrive with her camcorder. She seems delayed in coming, but then I hear the footsteps splashing in the water, which flows from the fall. However it turns out to be a man and his wife, completely unknown to me, who have come to see the waterfall. My heart sinks, and for a moment there is less joy in the cascading of the water and less beauty in what I see around me.

Trevor

Just as doubts begin to arise in my mind as to our relationship, she rounds the corner in the brook, and love and joy flow between us until not even the waterfall really matters.

Eventually we walk back to the car, and drive to a local hotel in New Radnor, where we enjoy a glass of red wine.

As I am taking her home, the car engine breaks down. We are miles from anywhere, I have not got my mobile phone and my AA membership card has just expired.

In the end we flagged down a passing motorist and he took us back to the same hotel, where we spent the night in separate rooms.

Michael D Lewis

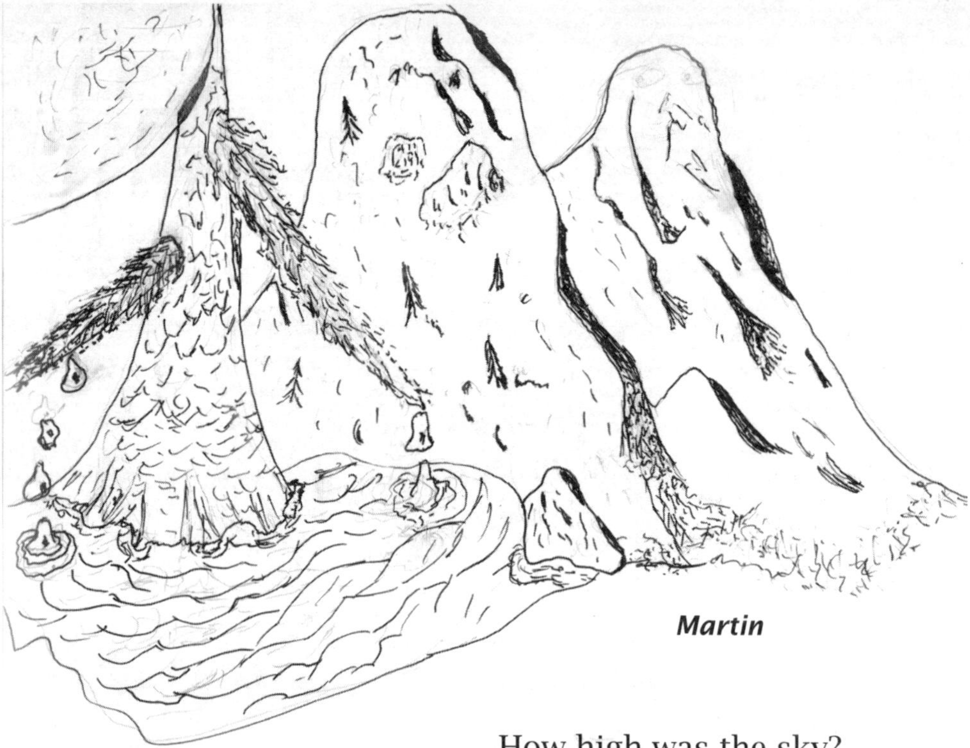

Martin

Touch the sky

I stood by the mountainside
and began to weep.
The oceans formed
about my feet.
The grassland grew with
sweet morning dew.

I raised myself up, all salt and
water spent.
I could not help myself I flew.
I passed the clouds, the snow,
the dream.
Rising higher than anyone
has ever been.

How high was the sky?

Bang
I hit my head on a
celestial sphere.
I feared that it would crack.

In starry gaze,
A silver moon became maiden.
My heart went boom.
Then she spat! Just like that!

I no longer flew
Gravity caught me
I landed in grassland
And washed my face in dew.

Gavin Pugh

Cariad

You are the strong tree
that bends but doesn't fall;
you are the endless running stream
that doesn't change at all;
you are the circling hawk
that comes before I call.

You are my Cariad, my dear,
my one and only for this coming year.

Pat

Ruth

If you will be my Valentine
To follow in the footsteps of the saint would be fine
Throughout February and the year beyond
our love would be a very tight bond
I think you know we would be admired
By our eternal warm glow it would be fired
Presents and cards would be things of the past
We'll know there is plenty of love in our hearts
Like spring our love would blossom with flowers
We'll be happy in each other's arms for hours
We'll be flying high like a bird on the wing
Our hugs and kisses will mean everything
Partners in love
Signed by a dove
I think we've landed with our feet in a tree
If only I could write fine poetry

Peter Munn

Ruth

I heard a lark rise from the meadow,
from where the morning mist just cleared away,
I thought of her carefree life,
untouched by the man made troubles of the world.

Peter Pickford

Im Eisplalst. (Skating Couple)

The sun sets slowly and the ice glows amber,
Showing the patterns of the patrons play.
The lamps are not yet lit
It allows the lovers yet a little dark.

The swoosh, scrape, scratch
Of skates faded hours ago
Just after they first stepped onto the ice.
When we held each other tenderly
Like lovers new to love life.

We dance as if in a ballroom, about to win first place,
He holds me from behind; his hand caressing my face.
Not too close or too hard. It lasts but a second,
But in my memory it will be forever etched in place.

I feel his grip in my wrist, my arm pushed behind my back.
I feel his warm breath brush my ear.

“What are you doing?”

A woman in black must see my distress and glides towards me.
He releases me and slides away.

I crumple, fall. Her hand reaches for me,
Eases me to my feet with great grace.

She doesn’t say ‘Are you alright?’
She says with a smile
“I’m Mary Jane Mathers.
Pleasure to meet you.”

Gavin Pugh

Song For A Unicorn

Here we go again
The roundabout's still spinning
Can't get off this
Magic carpet ride
No matter how I try.

I need a unicorn
Some innocence in a tainted world
An antidote to
This jaded cynical despair.

But they're the stuff of legends
A myth to warn us all these
Cold nights and colder days
A last desperate dream
To ward off poisonous reality.

Amanda Wells

That's L/W for you

I see no peacock with his silly trill
I see no comet with its frosty spill
I see no cloud with its anchor of ivy
I see no oaks or elms nor fallen creepers woods
I see no ants or elephants, no whales
I feel no seas or wet glass, no slime
no glass in Venice, no water in the glass
I fill no wells with tears, I drown no
men with weeping, I fear no man
of tears, I see no flames in eyes.
I pierce the dark to see the world
at no time on a clock, I am not
the man who saw the wondrous sights.
Who is the man who saw the wondrous sights.
I am blind to wondrous sights.
Anona

Oblivion Isn't Freedom

Do you feel you're in hell? With no-one to care,
In a bottomless pit filled with blackness.
Where every thought of escape brings despair,
Because someone's decided you're useless.

You ask, "what's the point?" there's no way out,
Though you're screaming inside, no one hears you.
Your mind's in a panic and you're stuck on a roundabout,
Spinning faster, can't breathe, so what can you do?

Falling, still spinning, it's hard to hold on,
Thoughts eluding and drifting around you.
The will to survive slowly feels like it's gone,
And the doors to oblivion, inviting you through.

Temptation's strong hands reaching out, almost touching,
If you go, do you think that at last you'll be free?
You have to decide if the price is worth paying,
For, if you surrender, then you'll just cease to be.

Please don't take that step, you haven't the right,
Try again to find someone who'll care.
You'll ask how I know? I too fought that fight,
I know how you'll feel, for I've been there.

The violence, the pain, and the constant abuse,
Accusations of which were unfounded.
Tormented by threats, being told I've no use,
Even told that I should be committed!

I was tired of hurting, living nothing but strife,
I was tempted to forfeit my being.
Then with anger I realised, I was worthy of life,
He was punishing me, for the guilt he was feeling.

Bobbie Davies

He

He chopped my mother's mahogany desk to feed his stove.
He sold my grandmother's cross to visit a whore.
He tore my German autograph books up to light his fat cigar.
He raped my Chinese doll.
He spat on the photo of my great grandparents.
He beat my head with my father's clarinet.
He pissed on my Persian rugs.
He wrapped himself in my great grandmother's mourning shawl.
He swallowed her jewels
And he kissed my Buddha.

Anona

My Room

This room is broken
Still heart of a silent home
Emptiness fills it.

Jill Dibling

A Song

When you're nervous and blue
In doubt what to do
Misunderstood too - Ssh
Don't say a word

Climb bravely and gently and peacefully
Life's mountain
Seek only God's will
Trust him and be still
Ssh - don't say a word

Margaret Yockney
A loved and much missed member of
Ystradgunlais Community Contact group

Hidden Secrets

Buried deep in unforgiving soul
A life of torment, black as coal
A solid mass of pain so foul
And just for fun guilt's on the prowl
Hiding secrets long gone bad
Tears unrelenting, it is so sad.

Hiding needs and wants with shame
Strategy and ploys, playing the game
Shut the window, lock the door
Important, safety first, that's the score
Keep others from ever pulling apart
The delicate strings of mind and heart

The hidden life of a child's pain
Are concealed compartments in the brain
The labels yellowed and worn with age
Are sealed and secured with blinding rage
Are bound up and closed with quaking fear
To prevent the torrent undamning here

The older the body, the harder to block
The feelings behind the barrier of rock
A fissure, a crack in the wall appear
It's too tough to keep up the solid veneer
A battle, a fight, keep buried the cry
So tired, the only thing left is to die.

Sue

The Funeral

A stifling stagnant air in a small room.
Outside roses, dying slowly,
Throw their petals to the earth.

People crammed into a silent room
Forced to talk, polite, chat.
Distant murmurs, a hundred bees buzzing.

Clink of china cups on saucers,
Random beat of rain on the window pane,
Greyness of night descends.

Voices grow louder as the teapot empties,
The overcast sky looses its sight,
Shadows creep from their hiding places.

The fading roses of the garden dance to the wind's melody.
Outside roses, dying slowly,
Throw their petals to the earth.

Tracey Friel

The Necklace Breaks

The string of pearls is severed
And each drops one by one
From that frail thread -
to be scattered and lost forever?
No, to be gathered one by one as
they fall.

Cynthia Mullan

You shall not go unsung

Autumn
The leaves are falling
The rooks are cawing
Laura is dying
There is darkness and despair

Spring
The buds are bursting
The birds are nesting
Laura is living -
In our memory

Our bodies are one with the living earth
Our being is the Light of Heaven
Death is our transformation
There is peace and harmony.

The four seasons
Embrace the opposites

Completeness is contained within
their dissolution and harmony
within their turning.
The wholeness of being
is realised within the eternal now.

Cynthia Mullan

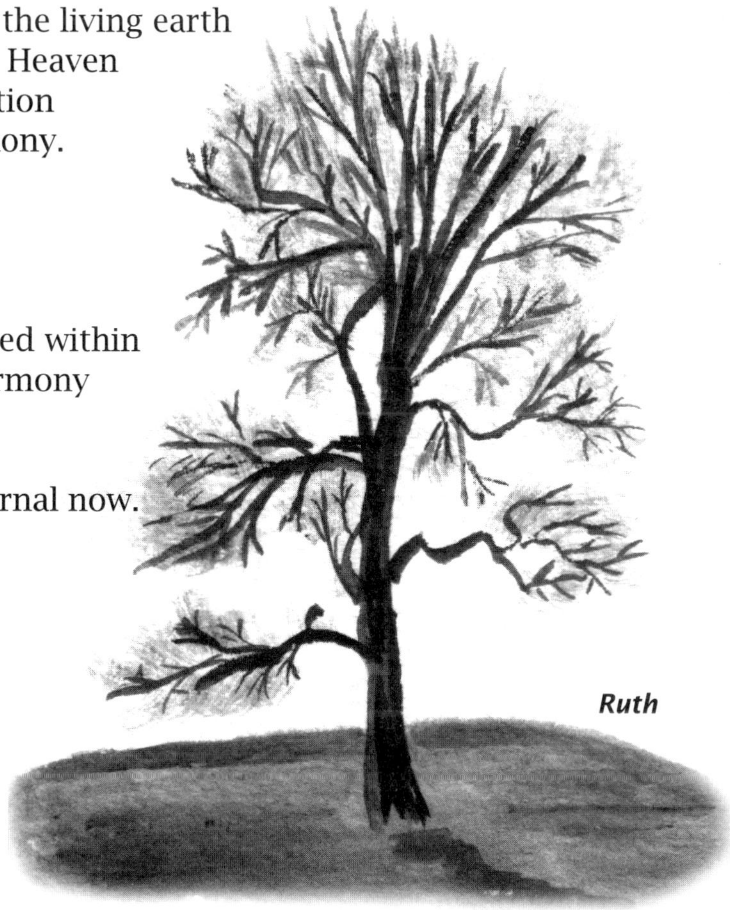

Ruth

Black Sunset

Once I had no one in whom to confide
The pain I was feeling kept hidden
I outwardly laughed, when inside I cried
I was locked in a world that was alien.

As these feelings took hold, I was drowning
In an ebony sea without light
And the deeper I sank, I stopped struggling
Too tired to think and too tired to fight.

Almost reaching oblivion, I welcomed its end
Then a sound broke the silence around me
A voice that was conscience spoke like a friend
And said to me, "don't you dare leave me."

"Would you go like a thief in the night
Steal away while the sunset is black?"
And I realised then, that I hadn't the right,
So I turned, for I knew, it was time to go back.

Bobbie Davies

I wish I could send a friend or lend a friend to somebody who needs friends or am I going round the bend.

When I am sad I'm mad and when I see my puppy I'm happy. I once lost my dog in the fog and found him sitting in a log. When I was stuck in a bin the smell was like being in hell. Oh, I'll have a bath. Oh it's not so bad and I'm not so sad anymore.

Only the sound of the waves gives me peace of mind when my head is fussy and mussy. I hear the sound of angels surfing on the waves.

I can hear the cries of anxiety as the waves hit the door. The squelch as the cars go by.

Robin Wilson

Crossroads

She ran into the darkness
That matched her aching soul.
This night that was the crossroads,
Had taken its terrible toll.
Such agony was painful,
She stumbled over stones.
The trees were blowing wildly,
Making creaks and groans.
The river flowed on temptingly
As she walked on by its side,
Confusion in her body
And thoughts raged far and wide.
The rain lashed down upon her.
She stopped and soaked up water.
Her shoulders quivered chillingly.
An awful feeling caught her.
But someone must have spoken
To her anxious form.
She turned and left the darkness,
To ease the inward storm.
Whatever happened to her,
She felt she had to meet,
To tap on any inner strength,
And walk with both her feet.

Judith Thomas

I buried it in the back of my subconscious mind. The experience had been so terrible that I don't even want to think about it again.

What I am talking about is one particular experience I had while detained at Mid Wales Hospital, Talgarth. I had been causing trouble on the ward, and I was forcibly injected (presumably with chlorpromazine) and then locked in a room.

What happened in the following hour or so was worse than anything I have experienced before or since.

However I am here to tell the story and I've got to look to the future and put all things like this behind me.

Michael D Lewis.

Mental Health Self Reforms (Part 1)

Breaking down the isolation, returning self esteem,
People sharing information, no it's not a dream.
Service users training others,
Professionals stand and stare.
Roles reversed, one soon discovers,
The buck does not stop there.
Everyone just work together,
It's important that we do.
Because those think they know it all
Just haven't got a clue.

Pash

Am I Pink Bicycle, A Hat Or A Mat?

Today I'm a pink bicycle,
Tomorrow a one wheeled tricycle
It tips and it shakes
And rude noises it makes.

Next week I'll be a yellow balloon,
Not oval, not heart shaped one just like the moon.
Children love me until I burst.
The burst balloon seems to bring out their worst.

I am a hat,
On Tuesday a mat.
I wear purple shorts
And break down toy forts.

I am inspired to maim and to kill,
But forget those ideas when I take another pill
I am ageless and mindless and don't give a toss
Perhaps Wednesday evening I'll conquer lacrosse.

Ruth

Pardon

Pardon! What did you say?

When was the last time you
Washed the kitchen floor?
The house is a mess,
The dishes not done,
Is that what you said?

I beg your pardon but don't you realise
How hard I worked today!

Pardon! What did you say?
I'm a dirty, lazy slob!
Is that what you said?

I beg your pardon, but don't you realise,
How exhausting it was just to live today!

Pauline Dean

Come Into The Shadows Of This Red Rock And I Will Show You...

The pain of waste paper lives
The blood that's absorbed by the rock.
The flashes of golden glow that show
Hope is material and not eternal.

I will have your pain
I will seek to show
How easily your life would go
If you waste the twenty-four hour day
If I were you I'd
Play or build or use your head
But instead you insist to veg
On soap operas non stop

Your blood the red rock will drink!
Every drop before you can think!

Gavin Pugh

I smell the night trees

I smell the night trees
smouldering, retching into
the smoky sky, the acrid taste
of tar and bones and hides,
so wasted, so spoilt by the
fires from Hell, the pyres of
shame, the wasted woodlands
of pine shattered by the blasts
of mortar rounds seeking
their home shot. Conflict after
conflict. I smell the night
trees burn.

Anona

The Demise Of Dick Discipline

His hair uncombed, his teeth were yellow and he had a runny nose.
Unshaven face, since falling from grace, stains decorated his clothes.
Yet I remember him thirty years ago, clever, disciplined and cool.
Dressed in black, no one answered him back
The headmaster of my school.
But they took away his dignity, when they took away his cane
Eleven year olds then laughed at him
His stern face reflected pain.
He retired early, but he wasn't the retiring kind
He's walked the streets of Cardiff for five years now
A clever man who blew his mind.

Pash

Screen Of Trees

The huge overgrown jungle whispered its dark secrets
to the menacing silence.
Danger lay
Waiting to trap the innocent in static time,
Filled with the horror of the coarse, rough phallic symbols
of torture.
Boundaries are crossed,
Safety is a neglected path.
Rooted in
the screen of trees, where sunlight never penetrates,
where hidden shame grows out of proportion,
where life has no meaning and
where the metallic taste of fear resides,
I
Still strive to hold on to my humanity.

Carol Loud

Young Unemployed

Sitting around street corners,
Nothing else to do,
Young, yet so despondent,
Feeling really blue,
What does the future offer,
What jobs are there in store,
What has the country come to,
There are no jobs no more!
And they get annoyed,
Yes they get annoyed,
Their ego dented,
And their dreams destroyed,
They never reach their goal,
They just end up on the dole,
Get out there girl and join the unemployed,
We've already had race riots in our cities,
Soon the unemployed will set the town alight,
Destroying, not creating,
What a pity,
But then the tension did not build up over night,
They became annoyed,
They became annoyed,
Their ego dented and their dreams destroyed,
They never reach their goal,
They just end up on the dole,
Get out there son and join the unemployed!!

Pash

Waste Of Space

What a waste
This shop so big
What a waste the empty space
With people living
On the streets
What a waste of space
We will squat it
Make it a home
With free café
And free food for all
When they come to
Get us out we will
Go in another one
What a waste of space.

Bob Lewis

Christmas On The Streets

I wonder what is behind that door
A warm fire to keep warm
With pretty lights upon a tree
And young children
Dance with glee
I wonder what it is like
With food and warm
Whence on this winter
Dawn I look and see
Them smile at their
Presents all around
And log fire on the ground.

Bob Lewis

Mary-Jo

Dance Of Water

The dance of water, like the is ageless,
flowing from the taps, ebbing and flowing on our shores
creating new inways in its path.
So old and yet so young, forever renewing itself
from the energies of the earth.
Water Water everywhere, and yet
it is one of our most precious commodities.
The beauty of the sun or moon casting its shadows on the water
almost like they are playing within the dance.
And though we will surely pass away,
the seas and rivers will forever flow,
never ending or beginning but as one small part of the circle of life.

Margaret Hardman

Ruth

Dance

We all know about waltzes, disco, ballet dances etc. But what about "Dance of Tunes". How many of us dance to everybody else's tune (family, friends, neighbours) authorities (work, government etc.) How many of you dance to your own music, do what you want? We all spend our lives listening and dancing for everybody else. So maybe today should be the day, when you start to dance for you, to do what you want, live this life for you and nobody else. Learn to say No. Also remember to be careful, because sometimes what you do also affects others in some way or another.

Margaret Hardman

Kate

You were my first friend
for we sat at the table together -
It took so long to eat.
The mountain with all its patience
looked down on us in our wretchedness.

Now time has passed
and we have looked long together
at the mountain.
We saw how the clouds come and go
across its face.
It taught us to live in that moment
Where there is neither happiness
nor unhappiness.
Now when the sun shines
it smiles on us in our detachment.

Cynthia Mullan

Ruth

The Samaritans

There are many lost and lonely souls
Who find a listening ear in you
As you fill the demanding roles
Of being a Samaritan, in lieu
Of a friend or of a caring other
Of a confessor for secrets dark,
Sometimes the role of sister or mother.
Maybe a ray of light, a little spark,
You lovingly give a miniscule of hope.
Without judgement you don't condemn.
With your tenderness' ability to cope
You are always there for each of them.
Day and night you sit and wait
For the desperate caller to ring
And pray for the suicidal before it's too late
And supply a lifeline on which to cling.
Alas sometimes a desolate dying one
Needs the voice of a caring in their ear
Who loves them even when death has won
Who will take their pain and hurt and fear.
Sometimes though a happier tale
Your kindness has brought the hopeless through.
You've helped give courage to the frail,
Please don't stop what you've chosen to do.

Sue

Who Is Right?

Who is right and who is wrong,
neither you nor I can say.
For if everybody is right, then
everybody is wrong
Nobody is wrong and nobody is
right
For like the child learning to
add up, until they learn the
rudiments of basic numbers,
and are shown how to count,
(2+2) will always make 5, or any
number they want.
For we are all at a different level
in life, and our won
understanding of what we see.
And what we perceive the world
to be, only comes from our
understanding of the
knowledge that we have
attained in life.
It is not enough to know
something, (we all know a lot of
things). But our understanding
of what we know can vary so
much from someone else's,
depending how far we have
travelled or progressed in life.
We all progress at a different
rate to others.
Therefore hence the saying
"What is right for you, is not
necessarily right for others".
Therefore nobody is right, and
nobody is wrong.
What I say to you is right for
ME, but tomorrow could be
wrong, because of my learning,
(my knowing), but that is not to
say that I have understood.
So therefore what I say
tomorrow could be different,
because I have had time to sit
and think, and become aware of
what it means to me.
With each experience we go
through in life, (although it
happens), do we understand.
Do we understand the effects it
has on not just ourselves. But
others around us?
Sometimes I think not.
So when you come into contact
with others that you disagree
with, or they don't agree with
you, remember they may be at a
DIFFERENT level than you, on
this path of life.

*Q: Who is right, and who is
wrong?*

*A: Nobody! For everybody is
right. The truth and the
understanding for them, is not
necessarily the truth and
understanding for you.*

Margaret Hardman

Marriage Conversation

This dark sadness
that lies between us
is more than just
the loss of passion
or discarded tenderness.

Across the dining table
we regard each other
as mere additions
to the plates and cutlery
ourselves
folded
and stiff as napkins
poised for the sally
of practised conversation
our empty words
embroidering the gap
between our separateness.

Dusting off our promises
we begin the supper
forgetting how we began.

Len Thomas

All Heart

Today
I bought lamb's hearts
for supper;
they lie there
on the chopping board,
thick and rubbery,
with dark clots of blood
protruding from inside.

Of course,
when you broke my heart,
it wasn't this sort of heart,
I had in mind at all,
but something soft and
suffering,
in Marks and Spencer peach,
hanging
on the bathroom wall,
forever out of reach.

But now I find,
the thick skinned hearts
I'm chopping with my knife,
remind
me
that I'm better off
with ambivalence in my life!

Pat Atkinson

Troubles To Pearls

The oyster lay on the deep seabed
Suddenly in trouble.
A speck of sand entered his shell
And he was seeing double.

Poor oyster felt the pain so much
But couldn't push it out.
It pricked and prodded him inside,
And he began to shout

"I can't go on like this!" he cried,
Becoming yet more sore.
He fought against this agony.
It beat him all the more.

Then all at once he had a plan
To deal with all the grit.
After a very, very long time
It didn't hurt a bit.

Instead of all the ugliness
That caused his irritation,
A lovely pearl was formed around
This awful tribulation.

I'd like to learn a lesson
From things I tend to foister
To turn my troubles into pearls
Just like the wise old oyster!

Judith Thomas

Mary-Jo

The Silver Fish

While sitting by the river,
I saw a silver fish.
She asked me what I'd give her,
If she granted me a wish.

I turned my trouser pockets out,
And found a lucky horseshoe
I held it up and gave a shout,
And prayed that it would do.

She clearly was delighted,
And said, "now what's your
wish?"
I mused a while, enchanted,
By that lovely silver fish.

I gazed into her eyes of blue,
And swore I would protect her.
So I begged her make my wish
come true,
That I might dwell beneath
the water.

She beckoned, me "come closer,"
I did so in a trance.
I was drawn into the river,
Without a backward glance.

So be warned, or have no future,
Should you be granted
just one wish.
Don't be drawn into the water,
By a lovely silver fish.

Bobbie Davies

Robin Wilson

How I Got Over My Fears

When I was ill a while ago there were quite a few fears, I didn't want to go out with people and couldn't cope to do every day things, for example shopping, helping my parents in the house, just wanted to stay in bed and do nothing.

After I had seen Dr. Bhakta up at Mid Wales Hospital, Talgarth, he put me on special tablets and I started to pick up again slowly. Then there were different events in Crickhowell to go to like concerts, coffee mornings and day trips. I had lost quite a lot of interest but after a while I started slowly getting back into action.

My weight was low because I didn't enjoy my food when small things upset me.

They started a Day Centre in the hospital grounds so I used to go on a Monday and Friday and did different things each week.
So I got on well. I travelled by ambulance or car at 9.00am and home at 4.30pm. We had our dinners there, a good choice of meals each time. It made a change to go out of the house, as three of us lived in a one bedroom flat for a long time, until I could have a place of my own, which took eight years.

In 1990 there were flats available. I was very excited when they gave me the good news. It took six months to do all the decorating and gardening the way I wanted it.

So that's how I got over my fears.

I have good neighbours if I need them for anything at anytime. All my visitors like my flat, so I was pleased to have it. I have done lots of things myself when I got better from my illness, which lasted a very long time.

Glad I don't have it again or for the near future.

Moira

My Prayer, I give to you

The gentle drops of the rain.
The perfume of the morning dew
The warm sun on your face.
The sweet melody of the song bird.
The soft tone of the autumn wind.
The sight of the evening moon.
The unveiling of the first
spring flowers.
The wonderment of the stars.
The comfort of friends who care.
The gift of love.
The gift of self love,
as well as self forgiveness.
The gift of joy as well as sorrow
without one you can not know
the other.
The hand that will help you when
you are feeling discouraged.
The gift of laughter, with the
words never give up.
Good health, good will, and inner
strength to deal with life.
Positive thoughts on your journey
throughout life.
And if no one has told you how
special you are today then let me
be the first one to tell you so
May your God be with you now
and forever more.

Lorraine Crawford

The Dream

**I set my dream
amongst the soft hills
lined with diamond streams;
but when the sun sinks low,
the green flesh shrinks,
the hard bones start to show
through the seams.**

**Then the crouching dogs
with ribs of rock and
bared stone teeth,
seem wild for ever
on the sheep shorn heath;**

**The rigid fox,
the bitter cold,
the harsher words,
the endless worry in the night,
might have been the end;**

**But even travelling
in the darkness with no light,
there's God there,
somewhere,
who guards my dream,
who brings it back to life.**

Pat Atkinson

My Confession

I am both a teacher and pupil who's taught.
I have my uniqueness yet share in your thought.

I hope to create with feeling and life,
and remove from my being the reason for strife.

I have been a daughter, a mother and friend,
but what other roles will I take before my end?

I wonder if there is a power beyond what I know
I feel it, can touch it, it's so strong, will it grow?

I know as the years pass I seem to know less,
I need to listen more, be aware more, and tolerate mess!

Ruth

The old boiled egg topping 60 winked at the spoon
and got told off by the knife that was stuck in my back
to get on with things because the bloody tea was
getting cold, and there was no Pat to do the washing up.

Gina

"...Is Just A Car"

Life has no reverse gear: no going back now dear!
Life has no accelerator, you can't control its speeds.
Life has no brake, you can't stop here.
But life has a steering wheel: you can control where it leads.

Gavin Pugh

Martin

Stone

I was once the silt that lay on the bottom
of the river, that moulded and smoothed
all the stones in its path.
That eventually with rain and storm edged
my way to the side, and was picked up by
a child and skimmed back into the river
from whence I'd come.

Margaret Hardman

I Am

I am a clock measuring Time;
I am a river flowing free towards the great sea;
I am a ship voyaging to faraway places meeting unfamiliar people
    Different places. Different faces.
I am a plane flying high in the sky –
surveying the landscape below me an all-seeing eye.
I am a truck in an endless road coming and going, delivering loads.
I am a dog keeping watch in a farm, with me around the crops and the livestock are safe from harm.
I am a cat roaming wild and free
I hunt by night, sometimes I bring my spoils back with me.

Steve Davis

I have a face but no eyes
I have two hands
but cannot hold anything
I have no beginning as such
I have no ending as such either.
I have a face but do not smile.

I am a clock!

Mo Steele

The Spinning Wheel

Wound and wound the thread she found
Spinning daydreams that did abound
The thread did weave with endless seam
As she did chance to dream and dream.

With every turn of her spinning wheel
With every loving turn she'd feel
Romance well up within her heart
The love and the thread never to part.

Phil Brown

Love

The taste of love is like expensive lipstick.
The smell of love is her French perfume.
The feeling of love is softness and strength.
The sound of love is as when she phones me up
and I know who it is before I answer the phone.
The appearance of love is like that of a rainbow.

Michael D Lewis

If I Could....

I'd make people share dreams, in a loving way.
Nice songs that makes them need friends to be
there, even if just on the telephone.
It would be nice to stand in the moonlight,
just to be there, doing things for one another.
Together listening, enjoying and having fun
together for good.

Sian

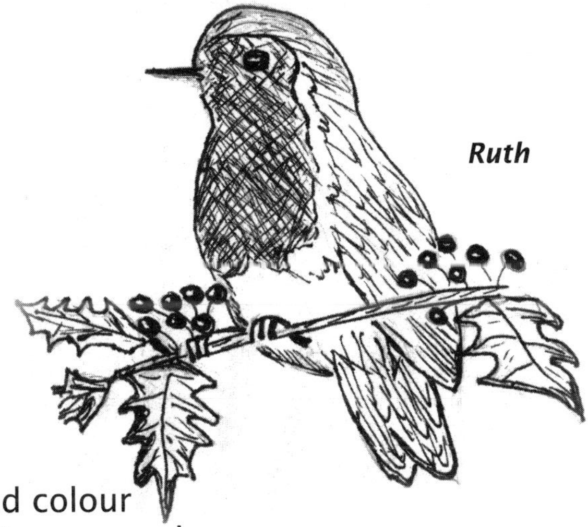

Ruth

Red

The leaves are turning a nice red colour
The holly berries at Christmas time are red
I saw a Robin standing on my gate and his breast is red
You can buy red candles
At Christmas you can buy red cards to send to friends
You can have a bright red fire
There are lots of red flowers in our gardens
There are lots of red apples in orchards
You can buy red string for gift tags
You can have red put in rings which people wear when they go out
I like red serviettes on tables for Christmas parties
Shopping bags are made from red materials

Moira

I am bright, I am used with amber and green.
I am a common colour; especially in car makes.
Everywhere, you go you see me.
I am on mugs, t-shirts, shoes, books, picture frames, posters and pictures.
I am the colour that is in everyone.
I am dramatic.
Without my colour in people they could die; - not saying that everyone will.

Mo Steele

Pig

The pig so red,
colour of dead,
colour of dried blood,
as it seeps from its head.

The taste of its meat
is really quite sweet
it's great with apple sauce.
You can eat it many other ways
but roast is best, of course.

My pig dreams of a long life
it secretly knows that each time it is observed,
somebody is estimating
how many cuts they can get for the most return.

When will I be ready for this ritual?
It dreams of food because it is always hungry
from dieting.

She's not a horse she has no saddle,
She's not a boat she has no paddle,
She's not a table that's made of wood,
She's just a pig and that is good.

I weigh more than a pigeon
less than a cow
I'm just an old pig, a dieting sow.

I'm a famous star sign in the Chinese horoscope
I can't tell you what that means,
I can't read, I'm a pig.

My origin is the ancient boar.
To some tribes I am the symbol of war.
I come from a time before man
I have changed over years into that which I am.

I am that which I am, sweet meat man.
I am that which I am, sweet meat man.
I am that which I am, sweet meat man.

The butcher is a man that I really fear.
I quake and I pee every time he comes near.

Anon

Blue

This is exactly the shade of blue that I have
been trying to replicate all my life:
Lapis Lazuli.
Virgin Mary's Renaissance veil.
Borage flowers in blue bloom.
Lightning bolt blue. Electric neon blue.
Photographic sky blue.
Budgerigar's bill blue.

Anona

Remembering Wishford Magna

On Oak Apple day, the men would cut boughs off the oak apple trees. They would run around the Village shouting.
"Grovely, Grovely and all Grovely!"
It was something to do with the right to cut down wood from the woods.
In the fields there were the dark green circles of fairy rings.
"Never step on the dark green grass, for that is where the fairies made their mark and danced."
I can remember a special day, like a procession with fancy dress. I was dressed as Mrs Mop.
"Can I do you now, sir?"
It was a long time ago
Its dell was on a farm up beyond Pentre Lane. There were tall standing trees and the dell's grass was deep, dark and soft. There would be carpets of bluebells everywhere. I remember the soft sap of their stems and the wonder of their scent. We'd walk '*up on the downs*' and pick cowslips.

Wishford Magna was never the same after I left.

Wendy Jones

Still

The door was shut, I looked between its bars and saw it lying still as the morning air, as quiet as its own last breath, its huge bulk still steaming, still warm - still. Everything so still, the chill of the day froze the tears on our cold cheeks. It seems that the only warm thing in this world was the steaming dead bull. All his marvel, all his breeding, all his bravery, all his mass, all his wonder felled - stilled - enstilled.

Anona

I am solid,
though not a rock.
I am man-made.
I can be a chip off the
old block.
I can be heavy.
I am very square.
I am not wood.
Though for making
things; I am very good.

I am an anvil.

Mo Steele

Guess Who?

I am as old as sand and light.

I speak languages of fairness and beauty,
but also of blemishes and blackheads.

I dream of a companion to watch
and wink to infinity.

I reflect on each moment,
but never on memories.

I am also known as: Quicksilver press,
Light skater, Image-maker.

I am always watchful,
I'd like to rest.

My secret is the blend of revenge
I will send to whoever shatters me.

My ambition is to store smiles and sparkles.

I'm afraid of damp, mildew and darkness.
And vampires who tease me.

I eat youth, time and light.

Chris Kinsey

Which Door To Enter

Ruth

An open door to the garden.
A closed door to the cellar.
The green door welcoming you
into "The Bell".
A sepia door, peeling, behind the
overgrown entrance to the
dilapidated large house.
One of the red doors in a back
street of Amsterdam
Red door, yellow door, blue door
in St. Albert's Terrace.
The large wooden door,
so heavy it runs on
rollers as it opens into
the confines of the
prison.
The tiny door with slit
for letterbox and
minute knocker on the
gaily-painted doll's
house.
The door that jams on
the stone floor each
time it has rained!
Each door holds a
secret, a new beginning
– which door do I enter?

Ruth

Ian Grade

The Mirrors

I'm a hundred and thirty six and I'm still going.
I speak all languages in all Galaxies.
I dream about objects all different shapes and sizes.
I reflect light and colours, reflect copy images.
I collect beams of light and rays.
My secret is to capture time in all the Worlds in the Galaxies.

I'm afraid of no sunlight or light of any kind
or no colours of rays and darkness.
I tell the truth of what I see.
I eat light energy, colour energy, energy of moving shapes.

Robin Wilson

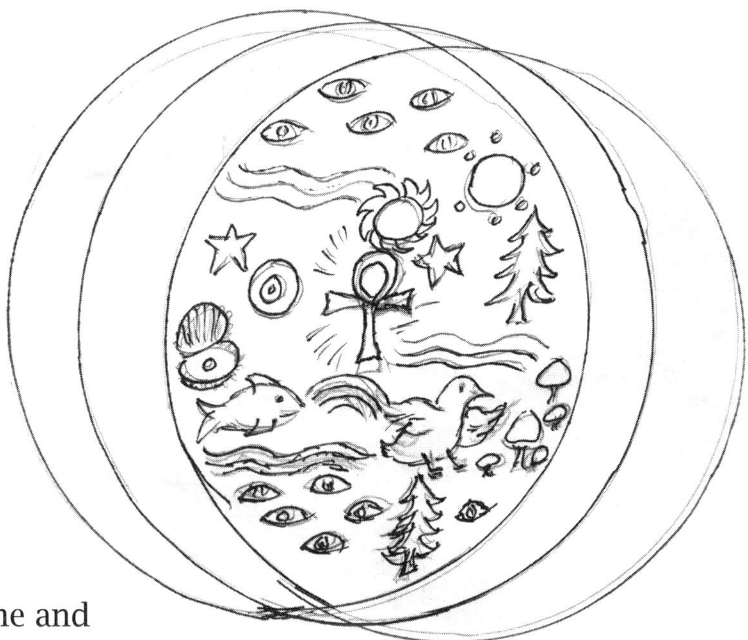

Mirror reflecting Time and Eternity. It dimensionally causes "shift" to the gazer. It is becoming what it reflects. All of life Terrestrial and Celestial seized. Reads Earth and Stars in its gaze.

SCRYING
TIME SHIFTING
THETA

Mary-Jo

The Beautiful Image

Sometimes the creature that I see is really quite a mystery, the things you do in this small room, I watch your ritual as you groom your wonderful body in the shower. Cold water splashes from which you cower. Lathered soap steam, I see a look on your face a luxury, you do strange things when you look my way, you do them each and every day.

Strange faces, positions "one might say you think you're the greatest thing today". There is of course the other side too. I see sometimes on the loo grotesque expressions as you pass it through the pain I see upon your face I wish I was hung in another place. I see you laugh, I see you cry. Removing grit blown into your eye, spots you squeeze puss hits my glass how I wish those spots were on your ass.

Anon

The Ring

You'll never believe it if I told you - this woman came into the shop and insisted on having me, I knew I wouldn't fit, I do know my own size. She struggled for a good ten minutes with the shopkeeper pleading that he had other more suitable rings. (By the way we rings never called ourselves that, it's such a human word)

Anyway, at length she possesses me and leaves the shop only to trip on the kerb and fall heavily into the road; with of course the little finger of her right hand extended full reach into the muddy roadway. Needless to say, along comes a cart and severs the bloody fingers clean off.

Well the fuss and cufuddle was and had to be seen. The woman from the shop was fainting, the woman upon whose finger I so recently spanned, lay bleeding at the hand and shouting for Charlie.

I on the other hand (if you will excuse the pun) was whisked away, finger and all by a young guttersnipe - probably to end up being sold for a tot of gin.

Anona

The Moon

I am about 200 million years old
or so scientists believe from my
Mother Planet. I have been here
in space so long that I don't
really remember.
I am familiar with all language
forms in this Solar System.
I think about the light I send to
Earth, my effect on the tides
and weather there.
Also the 12 men who have
walked on my surface and the
many space craft that have
landed here.
I dream about having women
and children visiting me, and
about a permanently manned
Moon base.
Also I dream about the people
from Earth extracting some of
my vast mineral and other
resources.
I am a satellite of Earth, there is
nowhere on the face of the
Earth where I am not seen, and
every tribe and people have a
name for me.
My secret is why my
gravitational field is abnormal.
I have no fears of any kind
I always speak the truth, always
have done and always will do. I
have got nothing to hide.

Michael D Lewis

Mary-Jo

MOON MAIDEN

A Long Time Ago

A farmer busy doing his ploughing, a hitchhiker oblivious to what's around him. A fisherman falling asleep with boredom, holding his fishing rod loosely. You can hear the prison alarms in the near distance but nobody is taking any notice, like it's a regular occurrence.

Two prisoners have escaped, Socrateze and his son Gabel. They have made wings out of golden wax and dived off the top of the prison walls waving their arms up and down at rapid speed. They look really silly. The day was sweltering hot with a light breeze at the north side of the wall.

Socrateze had advised his son Gabel to jump from the north side of the wall but Gabel disagreed with his father and jumped the west side of the wall.

Socrateze was jumping with the breeze but his arrogant son Gabel hit the hot blazing sun. Soon his wax wings began to melt and he nose-dived into the sea and to his death. As he could not swim he gasped and grabbed for anything he could but failed.

People looked, oblivious to what was happening. They seemed like ghosts not human beings.

Robin Wilson

I can hear a drum beat at NASA as the rocket or space shuttle takes off.
I can smell the vapour from the after burners.
I eat after burners for lunch and spit the hard bits at the moon to create the craters.
I have entire energy atomically in all matter, so I may as well move in a bed and breakfast in Neptune.
Eio=cd5 o + i sin o.

Love ecdove-ee poca mass dies bien.
When in space and you try to shave, the whiskers or bristles can float up your nostrils.

Mo Steele

Group Limericks

There was a girl called Rosy
Who at night slept exceedingly cosy
Then she fell out of bed
Hit her poor head
But luckily she landed on a tea cosy

There was a man named Simon
Who one-day met a pieman
They went to the pub
Ate some nice grub
Then Simon said goodbye to the pieman

A man with a hat named John
Said it's Talgarth where I'm from
I eat curry, drink beer
But soon I'll disappear
Come five o'clock - I'll be gone

There was a man called Bill
Who sat on a windowsill
I'm clever he said
Then he fell on his head
It made him feel dizzy and ill

There was a man called Phil
Who was faced with a very big bill
Instead of buying some grub
He went down the pub
Got drunk and then fell down the hill

Willow Centre Brecon

Group Limericks

A lady from Abergavenny named Anne
Drank Coca Cola out of a can
She drank Whisky as well
Tripped over and fell
The police took her off in a van

A creative sort of person called Gill
Was blessed with amazing skill
She'd paint and she'd draw
And yes, she did more
She made a mountain out of a mole hill

A lady from Talybont called Nicki
Each morning performed something tricky
She'd jump out of her bed
Stand on her head
And with one hand dunk her tea with a bicky

The was a man from Talgarth called Mark
Who went fishing in the sea, it was dark
To catch a big trout was his aim
It was such a shame
When he was eaten up by a shark

Brecon

The Little Hamburger

Once upon a time there was a kingdom of Hamburg, and all who lived there were called Hamburgers. The people were ruled over by the King who had a son called Romell.

The king made a proclamation to the people that they should take a certain quantity of hamburgers sufficient in total to fill the king's reserves, otherwise he would be unable to feed his countries. You see the people lived exclusively on hamburgers.

In her turn there came a young girl named Gretchen. When she arrived at the king's palace she was met by a sentry. She was asked, as was everyone, the same question which was, how many hamburgers would it take to feed all the Hamburgers in the Kingdom in a year?

All the pretty ladies before Gretchen tried hard to answer the question but could not do so, but Gretchen's answer was, "not too many and not too few." Her answer was a perfect example of common sense.

The king's proclamation was also intended to establish the most desirable Hamburger for marriage. Although the King was ageing, his vast estate and wealth made him an irresistible attraction. Gretchen, "the little Hamburger" amazed the sentry, who ushered her into the King's throne room where she was introduced to the king. The little Hamburger showed her willingness to marry.

Low and behold, the curtain behind the King's throne opened and out stepped Prince Romell. The whole exercise had been devised to find the ideal Hamburger to marry the Prince.

Gretchen and Romell fell in love at first sight and the King put forth a proclamation of their betrothal.

The whole kingdom of Hamburg enjoyed a feast in celebration and the hamburgers were enjoyed by all. Gretchen and Romell lived happily ever after.

Phil Brown

Dreams Made Real Turn Into Millstones

There were two sisters named Jocasta and Cassandra and they lived at the end of a rainbow. It was quite an interesting life, one way and another and they got to see quite a lot of the world.

It wasn't always convenient though as rainbows tend to appear and disappear quite suddenly causing disruption to many day to day activities. Of course it was sometimes a problem if they went out as rainbow's ends are notoriously hard to find and sometimes it took days to find their way home again.

They did however have their own crock of gold, which was very convenient with the benefits agency.

When they did venture out they always carried with them a picture of their own favourite rainbow's end. It was a photograph kindly taken for them by a photographer who specialised in taking snap shots to be made into postcards for sale in Aberystwyth.

It was quite a dramatic scene of the seashore under a dark and stormy sky. It showed them arriving home from a very good party in the hills above Machynlleth.

They particularly liked the way the picture drew the eye homeward around the bay.

As most people realise, rainbows only become visible in the right combination of sunlight and rain.

Jill Dibling

Ponthafren Boasts

Esme

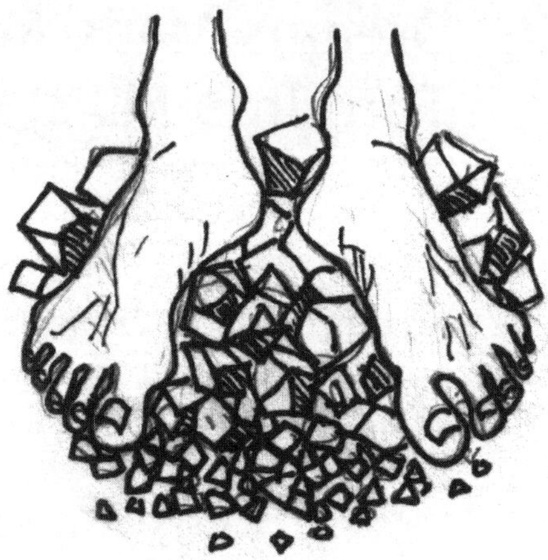

My feet are so flat I crush the garden rock
to make gravel for the paths
My hands are so big I can catch the sun.
When I walk up and down the stairs
things shake in the house
at the end of the street.
I stand on tiptoes and touch the clouds.
I'm so tall my hair gets tangled
in jet aircraft.
My mouth is so big it can accommodate the British naval fleet.

I can hear the dogs barking back at the house.
I can hear the echoes of wolves howling down
from the Arctic
I can hear the music made by mice in a tree
in the Australian outback.
I can hear a wombat fart in the eucalyptus forest.
I can hear a bluebell ring
in my aunt's garden in New Zealand.
I can hear Henry VIII belch from his grave.

Trevor

I can hear an owl hooting from the hills of Snowdon.
I can see an elephant flying over the moon.
I can see a polar bear wandering through the desert.
I can hear a seagull calling to the wind.
I can hear a flower petal opening to the sun.
I can hear the elastic twang
on the girdle of a singing nun
whilst diving for pearls in a long lost cave.
I can hear the oyster sigh
whilst it clamps its lips tight
and hides its pearl in its squish.
I can hear the wind which is so still
nothing moves to its breath.

I could race twice round the world
in the time it takes to pick your nose.
I can race twice round the world
with my two legs tied together
by the time you blink once.
I can race three times round the universe
with both my legs tied together
and my arms tied together.
I could pick my nose, blink,
race a million times round the universe
with my arms and legs tied in chains.
Well I can pat my head and rub my stomach
at the same time.
So, I can walk and chew gum
and I reckon I'm doing pretty well.

Ponthafren Group Poems

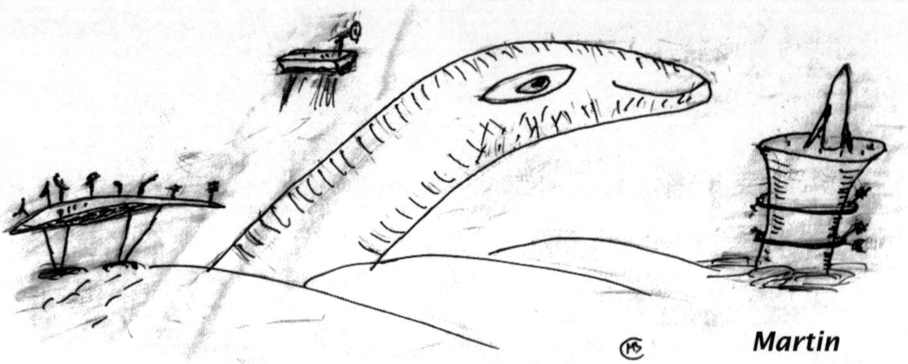

A Flubble Is A Wondrous Beast

It slinks seamlessly on all six legs.
Perfection in motion.
Its S shaped back moves as if
Motioned by the music of a snake charmer.
Though, a snake charmer would have to be brave if
He tried to tame this animal.
They're human in mind and soul
With a body that's totally under their control.

If you could get close enough to touch them
You would never want to let go.
Pleasure would tingle through your fingers,
Up your arms, into your soul.
The tiny hairs would waggle and tickle
And hook under your skin.

That's the catch they don't want you to go.
They're happy to meet you and then to eat you.
You'll see a human smile that would
Put the Cheshire cat to shame.
Their feline eyes would hold your gaze,
then wink and they'd purr.

They'd say softly in their aristocratic English droll
"So glad to eat you,"
Wrap a napkin around their neck and go.

Gavin Pugh

My Encounter

The machine opened its heart and cried. I was afraid to stop and look. What sort of machine was it? I've never seen anything like it before. It came down out of the sky. It was a dome shape with eyes for windows and legs for support. I started running and kept on running as fast as I could. But the machine hovered over me and then landed in front of me and opened its mouth. And out of this mouth came something not of this world or earth. It begged to come in but I was too transfixed and couldn't move my feet. It had three heads with three eyes on each head and about two tentacles. The tentacles were rhythmic in moving and when they came to grab me I was so scared I wet myself and blacked out. I awakened in my bed and the day seemed to have turned into night. On my walls were beautiful pictures of what I'd experienced which I cannot remember drawing or seeing.

Janet Moran

Martin

When Turtles Dance With Wrinkled Feet

They have no need to rhythm or beat.
Heeding some far off silent call,
they point their noses
 and make their haul.
In balancing breastplate
 on a sunny rock
they proceed to ballet
 with feet and neck.

Chris Kinsey

Mary-Jo

I rested at the foot of a tree
that seemed to sail into
infinity; occasionally leaves
would circle and spiral in the
gentle air currents and tease
the sun with its shadows.
A small silver child with ropes
of golden ringlets skipped
along the woodland path.
The little machine opened its
heart and I saw it take a cloth
and oil in its pigmy hand.
It wiped the metal object till it
shone, oiled it and returned it
to its chest. A tin rabbit with
crimson buttons for eyes
peered from a bush, winked
at me and disappeared down
a rabbit hole.
Speckles of brass ants
marched on the forest floor
ignoring the merciless sun.

Tracey Friel

Mountain

The conical peak stretching upwards mingles with the drifting clouds. The blue of the sky shades it to hues of purple as it stands majestic against the skyline. Snow covers its top for most of the icy season, whilst vibrant green coats its base in the season of blossoms.

Getting closer to its mass, there are contrasts of covering. Prickly gorse ablaze with flames of gold in the spring air gives way to thorny brambles and thickets with the mists of autumn.

Upwards ever upwards the smooth rocks provide a seat to the weary hiker, stretching out a hand to connect with the ageless beginnings before life. I am there on this mountain. My nostrils are filled with the air's freshness, skylarks rise overhead and I sit near the top and melt into the earth and sky.

Ruth

Sunflowers

I have stood alone amongst a
million, mad, waving, sashy
sunflower heads all turned like
golden soldiers towards their
own, one and only God, which
blasts down upon the pretty,
yellow slaves until their seeds
pop like corn in a pan, to end up
in a small, gold box here, a
million miles from my
sun-soaked birth with the
soldiers of sunshine marching
over endless scorched horizons.

Anona

When Turtles Dance With Wrinkled Feet (2)

When turtles dance with wrinkled feet
And dolphins crash the sea with a beat.
The sand turns red, the sea turns pink
Lobsters learn to write with ink.
The silver shoreline slips away
Scorched silver fish struggle and play
Into cool, dark, glassy rock pools,
Meanwhile octopuses glide like ghouls.
Among ship wrecks a thousand years old
Sharks cut through the seamless sea's folds.
Sun pierces the deep with its bars
And lights up plankton like sea stars.
Jellyfish sway like chandeliers.
Hopeful children cast lines from piers.
As the sun sinks into the sea
Night casts its shadow noiselessly

Tracey Friel

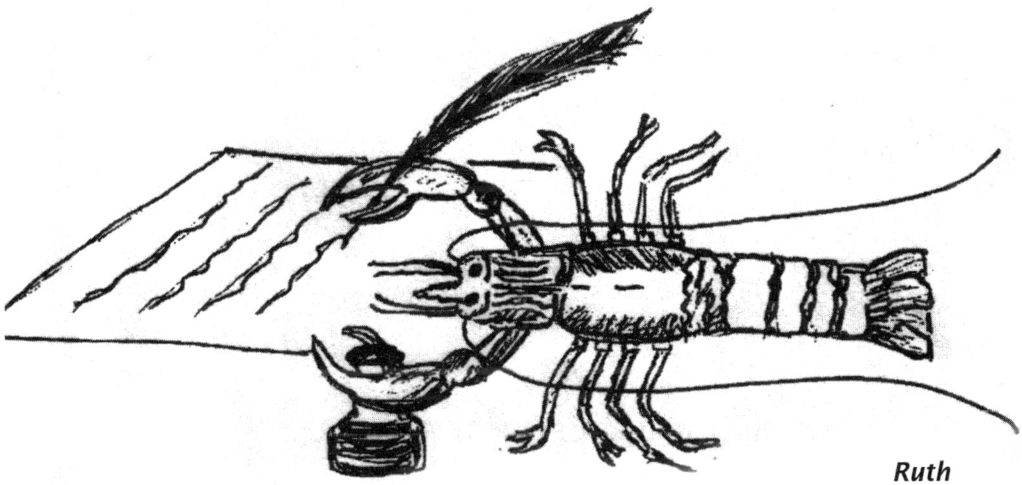

Ruth

Sow Thistle

A splash of sun
sweet to taste but sour to bite.
A crunching egg like shell of
sapping, savoury life.
Daydreaming of the honeybee
that spreads my pollen.
The nightmare of winter grows
and spreads
like an infection through my
mind.
I'm quite distraught at the ideas
people have of me:
I am not a weed.
I am not unfeeling
and I am not a dog's lavatory.
My head is heavy and my neck-
like stem
bends under the weight of my
golden crown.
My star sign is Cancer, the sign
of the summertime.
I originate from cool mother
earth and peer out
from her calm soils to bask in
the idle summer sun.
My only fear is the mechanical
monster with its slashing claws
that swallows my kind whole.

Tracey Friel

Narcissus

I am a yellowy brown bulb with
shades of darkness
As I bite into it the taste is sharp
and bitter.
My saliva yearns to spit it out, but
it's hard in company.
My object dreams of the nutrients
of the earth that feeds it,
to flower beautiful colours in the
hot Spring,
to show off my petals.
I'm not very tasty, but I'm good to
look at when I'm blooming.
I'm not to be trodden on
and I'm not liquid.
I weigh as five feathers
from a dove.
My star sign is Libra
because I'm happy
and content growing
at my own pace.
My origin is that I'm born
of the Earth
and live off the nutrients
and proteins of the Earth.
I am a purring bubble.
I am a purring bubble.
I am a purring bubble.
My aim is to fulfil my destiny and
show off beautiful colours.
I fear a giant worm may come and
take a chunk out of my side.

Robin Wilson

Ruth

Owl

Oh! How I Would Like To Be The Wise Old Owl Sat In A Tree Top,
Watching And Being Aware Of All Things,
With Its Plumage So Beautifully Layered And So Soft.
Talons So Sharp, To Kill Its Prey,
Yet Able To Pick Up Things So Carefully.
A Beak Sharp Enough To Rip Apart Its Kill.
Yet So Skilfully Used When It Comes To Picking Up The Young Owlet.
Eyes That Are So Perfectly Formed Into Its Face,
That It Gives The Impression It Can Turn Right Round.
Ears That Are Small In Size, But Can Pick Up The Slightest Sound,
Distances Away, Combined With Its Strength Of Vision That Does Not
Miss A Thing, As It Majestically Sits Almost In A Trance,
Taking Everything And Everyone In.
And Its Graceful Wing Span, Gathers All The Knowledge And Information
Around, But Never Dares To Whisper A Word,
Just For The Occasional Hoot, To Let You Know He's There.
Oh! How I Wish I Could Be Like That Wise Old Sage Sat In The Tree
Known As The OWL.

Margaret Hardman

Wondrous Insight

I saw a parrot with beautiful plumage
I saw a lion fierce and frightening
I saw a dog happy and free
I saw a cat with eyes of an angel
I saw a sky orange and inviting
I saw a white bright light
        and it was heaven to me.

Robin Wilson

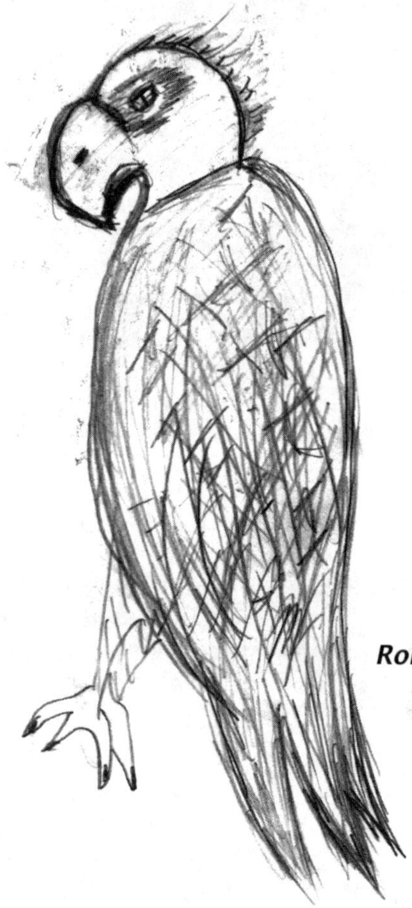

Robin

Rainbow

Rainbow fill the sky with your beauty
Join together the hillsides above the valley
Show off your colours to the awe filled children
Bring out the sun from behind your archway
Give your permission to the rain to fall gently
Fade slowly allowing your glory to linger
Come back again, and again, and again……..

Ruth

Robin

Ponthafren Group Poems

A Rising Sun

Do you ever think, oh no, why me?
Why do I have to wake everybody up?
Does an angel lose its wings
        and fall when you rise?
Why are you so bright and early
when I'm so sleepy and lazy?
Rising on what?
What happens when you burn out?

Ruth

Questions For A Rose

What colour are you?
Is it true that tears crystallise on your petals?
Are you tired of being the eternal symbol of love?
Was it red or white that caused a fight?
Subject of so much poetry,
do you need the thorn to remind us of your existence?

A Thistle

Do you relish drawing blood?
What sound would happen
If T was a double U?
Do you like to see your offspring
float away into distant fields?
Why are you so prickly as you stick into a hand?
Ouch!
How do you feel about being called a weed
When you're actually quite beautiful?
Where do you come from?
Is it true that the heart of Scotland lies within you?

Robin

Mary-Jo

A Viper

What do you think of as you slither
gently through the undergrowth?
Are you proud of your markings?
Is there anything as tender
as a snake's caressing kiss?
Why does such a silky, smooth creature like you
need to push venom into innocent children?
Why are you so fast when you attack?
Do you enjoy making people scream?
What are you waiting for?

Ponthafren Group Poems

Rain

I am ageless without beginning or end –
A universal sound varying in tone and tempo.
I'm busy nourishing the earth
giving life to the plants and flowers and the harvest crops.
I am the colour of the Earth –
grass, seas, streams and lakes.
I am water, dew, moisture and steam –
hot and cold and soft and hard.
The Earth absorbs me.
I arrive without warning
and stop when you least expect it.
I am afraid of nothing.

Steve Davis

Mosquito Magnified:

Eyes like domes of worship.
The original green-eyed
monster.

I'm blood-luster
A malaria-machine.

With trailing stings I come –

a full-frontal nightmare.

Just try to swat my wings
or silence my whine!

Chris Kinsey

Go inside a stone

I have been tossed on the seashore.
I have been rolled in the deep.
I have been thrown into darkness.
I have dwelt in a drawer.
I have been kept in a sea chest.
I have been dropped in a fishtank.
I have been sat on, spat on
And fetched up on a lap.

I was the stone that felled Goliath.
I was the stone used to
hammer the nails into the hand of
Man the Sacrifice.

I will be the stone to stone all stones.

I am stoned.

Anona

Associations

There was mud on his shoes so where had he been she wondered? Who was he? Who was she? Were there others? Who can say?

The first object reminds me of a plutocrat's Easter egg - an executive toy.

The second object is a beautiful cone. I have several at home which I found at a jumble sale!

I keep them in a brass coal scuttle.

A horse - what springs to mind is a 'horse a horse my kingdom for a horse?'

A mountain is there to be climbed up or skied down.

The sea - a rolling wave - birds - sand - the sky above. The only bit missing is the fragrance.

Pat Pritchard

The Helpless Whelk

Tumbling this way and that, lurching back
being sucked down and thrown up. I wish
I'd never let go in the first place but
there you go, go with the flow.

Spit out the grit, don't inhale
whatever you do. Wait for a lull,
for a break, then, get a grip.

Rocks fly past fast, I'll keep my
head down. Try not to drown.

Suns warm on my back - oh God,
think I'm going to be beached.

Ponthafren Group Poem

Things That Startle

A sudden change in tempo and dynamic in music.
Splashes from the quarry lorry.
The realisation the black stylish dress
contains a man in high heels.
Nessie waiting on the bank for swimmers.
Someone coming up from behind and tickling you.
A china cup deciding to drop onto the stone floor.
Salmon leaping.

Ponthafren Group Poem

It's Not Early Really!

**It's soon to be Christmas, let's have some nuts,
Then we'll hang up the holly and the ivy.
Let's practice our carols like a choir of cats,
'Till we scare all the bats in the belfry.**

**Some say it's early, so give us a break,
But already there's talk about Easter.
And some silly buggers have packed what to take,
For the holiday booked next summer!**

**So it's not early really, start swamping the shops,
Choose your gifts, and your turkey and stuffing.
Don't forget grandpa's Metz, or your Gran's alco-pops
Or the Chippendale for Great-Granny's stocking.**

**Oh I forgot, what was it you wanted?
Don't be shy, you can tell your old mam.
I don't think you're too old for a superman bed
So you're sixty; so who gives a damn!**

Bobbie Davies

Ponthafren

A warm glowing fire surrounded by Christmas decoration hanging from the ceiling, the low beamed room and bay window give a welcoming feel to the place.

As I sit here on this December afternoon felling warm and comfortable, cars and lorryies whizzing passed the window. People busy shopping or maybe just stopping on the bridge to watch the ducks on the river below. The air is clear and with it an embracing wind. A smell of mustiness fills the room of this old house, a house that is over 200 years old or there about. It makes me want to sit and drift with her, the type of people who first lived here, the architect who first designed and built this grand old house. What sort of people were they? What tools and instruments did they use? The gardens that once reached down to the park now reduced in size. The river continually flowing, never ever changing.

This house has seen so many changes from the days of the horse drawn carriages to the invention of the bicycle and later the car. The servants quarters below, with all the different bells going through to each room, this has all gone now. NOW you use your imagination to think what things would have been like in this great old house. Very grand, I should imagine with its stables, carriage and tack room, even grooms quarters at the top of the garden. I feel so sad, that such a beautiful house has been so badly neglected over the years, that it needs so much work to be done. That like the garden that once was so long and spacious, the house is going to change so much because there is so much work to be done I pray it doesn't lose its character and charm.

Tony Beswick

Margaret Hardman

Father

A large beak like nose dominates the face which is small. Smooth veined skin stretches over his bones but it is feathered around the eyes. Heavily lidded hazel eyes, swept by long fair lashes, are sunken into the face. His smile is still cheeky as if he holds a great secret. Very fine silver hair replaces the dark curls of his youth but it is a feature of which he is very proud despite his great age. He has difficulty speaking, not only collecting his thoughts together, but his frailty restricts the communication he desires. As he looks down deep veins protrude over the small bony hands gnarled by arthritis.

If I had a magic box to place treasures for his delight what would they be?
His tandem, and with it his youth, bracing air, and leafy lanes to cycle with his life long companion.
His wedding and golden wedding photographs, with all the good and sad years in between.
His darts so that he can be captain of the darts team again, visiting familiar jaunts with his mates.
A pint of Guinness to quench his thirst but will never quench the twinkling of his eyes.
The old box camera to produce a black and white glimpse of yesterday's past wherever and when ever he chooses.

Ruth

Esme Corfield

Esme Corfield

Just Before The Sand Grain Hit

I saw a child naked at play
I saw a swan roasting on a spit
I saw a butcher grin as he cleavered a kill
I saw a mountain wake without a sound
I saw a lemming following a sheep
I saw an electric chair burn a soul skin.
I saw a mouse swallow an elephant pill.
I saw a rat eat at a wedding cake.
I saw a funeral where the dead rose again.
I saw a smile sing from an eye.
I saw a pensioner killed by a goose.
I saw a phoenix crumble into ash
I saw a crocodile shoe bite off a leg.
I saw a bitter deer walk on two legs.
I saw a rainbow fall, killing a courting couple.
I saw a river on fire give salmon to the homeless.
I saw a coffeepot pour out tea.
I saw an angel trip a man on crutches.

Gavin Pugh

Ode To A Computer

In the early days I thought I was quite bright
I learned to read and I learned to write
Getting older I became "even brighter"
Using a portable, then electric typewriter
Then I discovered I was totally wrong
As the computer came along!
One day on the screen came the following information
"Go back to your typewriter - you're the wrong generation".

Pash

My Solicitor

Bald Bastard
Brief case
Legal beagle
Round face
Fast car
Friends at the bar
Got it made
On legal aid
Lawyer's life
Expensive wife
Old ties rule
Smells of public school
Shiny teeth
Brilliant brief
I shouldn't scoff
He got me off!!!

Esme Corfield

Pash

The Crying Came

I don't know why, that this moment in time
should be called life.
What's it all about anyway.
We cry for love gone,
we dream of that majestic love yet to come.
Cry for children born, not born.
Cry for childhood past, never had.
Cry for teenagers that should be, can't be.

Sleep with tears, hoping to forget, yet still we
wake up with that boundless liquid still stationary
on swollen eyes.
Existence seems to be full of tears, yet still we try
to find moments of tranquillity that will comfort
us in our time of lamentation.

Every day we are met with people who throw
assaults into our pathway of life, they say what if,
can't do, maybe some day you will, don't worry
things will get better they don't.
What they are saying is don't tell me your problems, piss off.
We spend so much time trying to work out
the meaning of life that we miss out on it,
we forget to get on with life, enjoy it.
We wait for the big event to happen
It does not draw near.

I wonder why this moment in time is called life.
Then I see a child smile and think maybe this is the promise of
things to come.
With that smile comes our hopes, our dreams,
Our future.

Lorraine Crawford